Phonics Poetry

An Anthology of Funny Poems for Decoding & Fluency Practice

by Lorrie L. Birchall

For my amazing parents,
Al & Le Ann Moore

Thank you to the following very talented morgueFile photographers for their wonderful photographs:

p. 8	"My Hamster"	(Snapit)	
p. 8	"I Had a Flabby, Tabby Cat"	(Alvimann)	Uruguay
p. 11	"Palm Tree Coconuts"	(albertinis69)	
p. 13	"Autumn"	(mconnonors)	New York
p. 14	"My Scrawny Little Puppy"	(xandert)	Arizona
p. 15	"May I Play Outside Today"	(iclipart photo)	
p. 16	"Winter's Blanket"	(kconnors)	New Jersey
p. 18	"Chester Chipmunk"	(AcrylicArtist)	
p. 21	"A Crab"	(iclipart photo)	
p. 21	"Crocodile"	(iclipart photo)	
p. 24	"The Centipede"	(xandert)	Arizona
p. 25	"The Eager Little Beaver"	(luisrock62)	Argentina
p. 27	"I Love My Little Gertie"	(matthew_hull)	Connecticut
p. 28	"Stew"	(alcinoe)	
p.29	"Flirting Flowers"	(ajjoelle)	
p. 29	"Snowflakes"	(Karpati Gabor)	Hungary
p. 30	"Frannie"	(iclipart photo)	
p. 31	"Glowing Eyes"	(Lazy_Lobster)	
p. 33	"Grasshoppers"	(earl53)	New Hampshire
p.36	"The Moon Up High"	(ardelfin)	Mexico
p. 40	"An Elk"	(rjshiflet)	
p. 40	"Why Do Cows Have Polka-Dots?"	(mensatic)	New Jersey
p. 42	"Frank"	(Schnuffel)	Germany
p. 43	"Otter and Frog" Otter	(monosodium)	United Kingdom
	Frog	(iclipart photo)	
p. 44	"Elephant's Nose"	(iclipart photo)	
p. 45	"All Aboard!"	(ancientecho1)	
p. 46	"My Worm is Not a Noisy Pet"	(DugganArts)	
p. 49	"I Should Have"	(iclipart photo)	
p. 51	"Howie"	(Karpati Gabor)	Hungary
p. 52	"Snow Day"	(ZeroSilence3)	Canada
p. 52	"The Crows"	(oOoOxmodsOoOo)	Florida
p. 53	"My Good Boy, Roy"	(phaewilk)	Virginia
p. 62	"The Spider"	(Jusben)	United Kingdom
p. 62	"Aspen Tree"	(Taliesin)	Arkansas
p. 63	"Astronaut"	(click)	Ohio
p. 70	"Burt"	(Taliesin)	Arkansas
p. 74	"My Parrot"	(mike)	Kansas
p. 75	"I Have a Lucky Penny"	(dhester)	Georgia

Teachers are granted permission to photocopy poems from this book for use in a single classroom only.

Illustrations are licensed from iclipart
Photography is courtesy of morgueFile and iclipart

ISBN-13: 978-1481184540
ISBN-10: 1481184547

Table of Contents

ă

My Hamster

My hamster sat inside my hand
to have a little snack,
but when she clamped down on my thumb,
I put my hamster back.

I Had a Flabby, Tabby Cat

I had a flabby, tabby cat
that sat across my lap.
He never moved all afternoon
when having his cat nap.

Crabby Max

Crabby Max was acting mad
and ran fast down the path.
His dad was simply asking him
to get into the bath.

ā (silent e)

Skates

I made a trade with my friend Kate
to get her purple roller skates.
I laced them up to have a race,
but faster Kate came in first place.

Snake

Inside a little crate
I placed a little snake.
I know that it is tame
because it is a fake.

Mother's Vase

When I broke my mother's vase
I wanted to be brave.
I didn't take the blame with grace—
I blamed my brother Dave.

-ai/air

Abigail, the Tiny Snail

Abigail, the tiny snail
went out into the rain.
She made a pail into a boat
and sailed right down the drain.

The Lair for Bears

A girl with pigtails in her hair,
went inside a lair for bears.
She sat upon a little chair,
and shattered it beyond repair.

The bears came home from their affair
to find a mess inside their lair.
The bears complained into the air,
"This is so mean and so unfair!"

When Baby Bear first saw his chair,
he felt so sad and in despair.
Then Goldilocks ran down the stairs,
and quickly left the lair for bears.

Palm Tree Coconuts

Palm tree coconuts
falter in the trees,
fall like giant meatballs
in the calming breeze.

Tall

I am very, very small.
All I want is to be … TALL!
I mark my height up on the wall.
Oh when, oh when will I be tall?

-ar

Carl the Shark

I'm Carl the shark,
I swim far in the dark,
looking for things to eat.
Don't be alarmed!
There's no harm in my charm...
unless you become my treat!

Inside My Magic Tree Farm

Inside my magic tree farm
I start to make believe—
The tree bark is dark chocolate
with candy bars for leaves.

Clark

You are the smartest puppy,
You hardly ever bark,
But when I take you to the park,
You always leave your mark!

-au

Autumn

In autumn leaves do somersaults
when launching from the trees.
It's automatic every year
before the winter freeze.

A Leprechaun

A leprechaun named Shaun McGlaun
was flaunting all the rules.
He acted very naughty
when he taunted kids at school.

-aw

My Scrawny Little Puppy

My scrawny little puppy
has one awful little flaw.
She gnaws on all the tables
with her teeth of little saws.

Seesaw

I saw a tiny seesaw
for a tiny little prawn.
It seemed a little awkward
when it crawled up to get on.

-ay

May I Play Outside Today?

May I play outside today?
I ask you in the sweetest way.
But "No!" you say—I cannot play.
Inside is where I have to stay.

You say it's time I put away
the toys I played with yesterday.
I like my toys out on display.
I only tripped on *one* today.

Okay...okay, I'll put away
the toys I played with yesterday,
if that is still the *only* way
that I may go outside to play.

Yesterday I was a Ray

Yesterday I was a ray,
Today I am a shark.
Imagination on display
when playing in the park.

-bl

Winter's Blanket

The blinding blizzard taking hold
becomes a blasting, blight of cold.
It blows into a blurry show,
as winter's blanket starts to grow.

Blueberries

I put berries in a blender,
I didn't use a lid.
I made a blender blunder—
Now I'm a big blue kid.

A Brooding Witch

A brooding witch fell off her broom
and broke her brittle nose.
She made a brew to fix the break,
but now her nose just.........grows.

Breakfast in Bed

I bring my mommy breakfast,
some bread with apple jam.
My brother brews her coffee,
and makes her eggs with ham.

-ch

Chester Chipmunk

Chester Chipmunk chews all day,
any food that comes his way.
Chili dogs and chocolate chips,
he can munch with chestnut dip.

Cherry pits, a chocolate treat,
he will always choose to eat.
Chunky, funky cheddar cheese,
he can chew up in the trees.

Chester fills his cheeks with more,
It's his very favorite chore.
In the branches he can crunch,
happy that it's time for lunch!

Duck and Chicken

Duck and Chicken planned to race
around the farmer's track.
Duck put on some lucky socks,
and Chicken packed a snack.

They started with some jumping jacks
and quickly ran the track.
Chicken ran with a cluck, cluck, cluck—
Duck ran quack, quack, quack.

They clucked and quacked around the track
till both were tuckered out,
but Chicken was the winner picked,
which only made Duck pout.

So Chicken gave her snack to Duck,
some peanut cracker jack.
They stuck together, friends again,
and quickly waddled back.

-cl

Clever

My mother says I'm clever
when I clean up with a broom,
or put away my dirty clothes
or clear my cluttered room.

I simply want to clarify
from now until forever,
There's clearly too much work involved—
so never call me...clever.

My Clue's Clunker

Mr. Clue must cling onto
his clacking steering wheel.
His clunker from the junker
was a most amazing deal.

When people hear the clunk, clunk, clunk
that's clopping down the street,
They clear a path for Mr. Clue—
and closely watch their feet.

I Made a Creepy Creature

I made a creepy creature
with some crackers and some gum,
until my cranky sister
crushed my creature into crumbs.

A Crab

A crab was crawling by the sea
and crashed into a wave.
He never cried or cracked his shell—
a crusty crab most brave.

Crocodile

The croc is very crafty
as he crouches in the creek.
He cruises under water
while his eyes have just a peek.

-dr

Dragon Dream

I drifted off to sleep one night
and had a funny dream.
A dragon drove me to my school
and dribbled on my team.

Drenched

I'm getting drenched in drops of rain,
It's dripping in my eye.
I'm feeling drab in dreary wet—
I miss the feel of dry.

ĕ

Greta's Eggs

Greta laid ten eggs each day,
Her nest was tended well.
The problem was that every egg
was empty, only shell.

When Greta went with Farmer Jed,
The hens could guess her fate.
Without fresh eggs, she met her end
as chicken on a plate.

This sent a message to the hens
who tend their nests so well.
It's better to lay one fresh egg
than ten with empty shells!

Spelling Test

I took a test on Wednesday
to see if I could spell.
I wrote the word that I know best—
and spelled it I-s-a-b-e-l.

23

ē (silent e)

The Centipede

The centipede will persevere
when crawling quickly over here.
With many legs he can compete—
He is a tiny bug athlete.

Eugene

Eugene is quite a cat serene,
His shape is like a sphere.
He will concede he is obese,
with fur of soft cashmere.

The Creature

There is a creature on my street,
and all he does is eat, eat, eat!

A heap of lunchmeat, greasy fries,
peanut butter, steaming pies.

Every meal is so appealing,
My dessert I fear he's stealing.

He just can't cease his constant feast,
He really is an eating beast.

There is a creature on my street—
my teenage brother, hungry Pete.

The Eager Little Beaver

The eager little beaver
will sneak across the wake,
and heap each log upon the dam,
to make his peaceful lake.

-ee

The Bleeks

Heed me when I tell you this:
Do not feed the Bleeks!

If you feed them, you will see,
You will need to quickly flee.

Speedy Bleeks have sixteen feet
and they will chase you down the street.

They will seek you out all week—
just to KISS you on the cheek!

Heed me when I tell you this:
Do not feed the Bleeks!

Sleepy, Sleepy Queen Doreen

Sleepy, sleepy Queen Doreen
liked to sleep all day unseen.

Deep in sleep she did not see,
She was sleeping up a tree.

She awoke to cheep, cheep, cheep—
Then she went right back to sleep.

I Love My Little Gertie

I love my little Gertie,
she is my perfect pet,
although she may be odder
than some other pets you've met.

She is an expert crawler,
an expert eater too,
her hunger for the flowers
makes her fatter with each chew.

I put her in a little jar
to keep her close to me.
I want to see her turn into
the butterfly she'll be.

I love my little Gertie,
my caterpillar pet,
but when she needs to flutter,
her freedom she will get.

-ew

There Was a Boy Who Liked to Chew

There was a boy who liked to chew
his bubble gum all day.
His bubble grew and grew and grew—
until he blew away.

Stew

I grew a few ingredients
and threw them in a pot.
I knew just how to make a stew
delicious piping hot!

Flirting Flowers

Tiny buds of flowers
flirt only with the sun,
then flash their flaming petals,
and flirt with everyone.

Snowflakes

Flocks of snowflakes way up high,
fly as flurries in the sky.
Fleece is flowing more and more—
floating to the snowy floor.

-fr

Frankenstein

My freaky friend eats frequently
on frozen fruit and pies.
When Frankenstein looks in my fridge,
I freely give him fries.

Frannie

Frannie is from Paris, France
with freckles on her face.
On Friday, she will frolic in
her frilly frocks of lace.

Glitter

I'm glad that I had art today—
I put on globs of glue.
I glazed the page in glossy white
before the glitter flew.

Glowing Eyes

Gleaming in the dark of night,
I glimpsed his glowing eyes.
My gloomy cat was glaring at
my glorious surprise.

-gn

Beware of the Gnashing Tree Gnome

Beware of the gnashing tree gnome
inside of his gnarly tree home.

He gnashes on gnats
in his tree habitat.

He gnaws on the gnus
which he chewy, chew, chews.

He reigns in the pine,
so look for his sign—

Beware of the Gnashing Tree Gnome!

Beware
of the
Gnashing
Tree Gnome!

My Grandma Grace

My Grandma Grace is cooking on
her very greasy griddle.
If you're greedy with her gravy,
you'll grow thick around the middle.

Grasshoppers

Greedy little hops of green
will eat the growing grains.
They never show their gratitude
when grazing on the plains.

Mr. Gruff

Mr. Gruff is such a grouch,
He likes to gripe and groan.
He grumbles when he greets you—
It's no wonder he's alone.

Ĭ

Sick

My skin is chilled, but I feel hot.
I cannot lift up from this spot.
If I move, I feel so stiff,
I have the sniffles when I sniff.

My head is spinning like a top.
It never feels like it will stop.
I sip my milk and pick my food,
I will not giggle in this mood.

I drift into my silky quilt,
and feel my body start to wilt.
I am not kidding, it's no trick,
I feel icky when I'm sick.

Jim

Jim is swimming in the trees,
His grip is never limp.
It's thrilling drifting branch to branch—
if you are a chimp!

Mice in Line

A wise old cat shined up a slide—
and five white mice lined up to ride.
The wise old cat had seemed so nice—
until he dined on five white mice.

Crocodile Smile

Please be careful of the reptile
and his crocodile smile.
He's trying to invite you in
his water domicile.

If he glides right up beside you,
then remember to recite,
His smile gets a mile wide—
just before he bites!

-igh (ī)

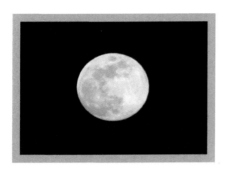

The Moon Up High

The moon up high
can shine so bright,
just like a light bulb
in the night!

Frightened

I get so frightened in the night
when monsters know my scary plight.

An alien might come for me,
and goblins might not let me be.

My sheets are right up to my chin,
and tightly held around my skin.

A nightlight makes my room too bright—
and helps the monsters see me right.

I wish I had a fighting knight—
to fight my monsters in the night.

Bring Me Spring!

It's holding umbrellas
and walking in mud,
and hearing bees buzzing
and peeking new buds.

It's hearing birds singing
and chirping to tell,
and seeing chicks pecking
right out of their shells.

It's picking red tulips
to bring to my friend,
and running with kites
and playing pretend.

It's singing and blowing
the wind in my hair,
and swinging on swings
in the cool, fresh air.

Bring me spring!

The Dragon King

The dragon king has little wings
but needs a giant hose.
For when he springs into the air
the fire stings his nose.

Oh, dragon king, you poor, poor thing!
That must be so embarrassing!

37

-kn

The Knitting Knight

The knitting knight had quite a knack
for knitting with delight.
He liked to knit his soft kneepads
so he could kneel at night.

The knitting knight knew even more
than knitting for his knees,
He liked to knit his knickers too,
his favorite dungarees.

The other knights acknowledged—
The knitting knight was right.
He was the only knight to kneel
on grassy knolls at night.

-lf

A Little Elf was Golfing

A little elf was golfing on
his lucky golfing hole,
until his ball was pilfered by
a selfish little mole.

On My Shelf

I keep some toys up on my shelf—
a spotted cow and Christmas elf.
Imagination is the best—
when I'm playing by myself.

-lk

An Elk

An elk was walking all alone—
majestic, hairy hulk.
He liked to stalk the apple leaves,
and eat them up in bulk.

Why do Cows Have Polka-Dots?

Why do cows have polka-dots
when milk is chalky white?
Do cows walk proudly with their spots,
or do they sulk at night?

-mb

Thumbelina and Tom Thumb

Thumbelina was a girl
no taller than a thumb.
She turned a shell into a spoon,
but only ate a crumb.

Thumbelina met a boy,
and he was called Tom Thumb.
They both had very tiny limbs,
so they became good chums.

Thumbelina had a pet,
a tiny little lamb.
They climbed up on his fluffy back,
and rode him like a tram.

Dumb Ideas

My brother has some dumb ideas
that keep on getting dumber.
He put a stink bomb in the sink—
We had to call a plumber.

He put some goop on top my comb,
and filled my bed with crumbs,
but you should hear the dumb ideas
my brother has for gum.

-nk

Donkey

Donkey drank a pinkish drink
that made him shrink and shrink.
Now he has to bunk inside
a dinky little sink.

Frank

Frank may be a little skunk,
but he can make you blink.
When he lifts his chunky tail—
he makes a great big stink!

Otter and Frog

Otter got on top a rock
to see his friend the frog.
The rock was hot, so they hopped off—
and swam across the bog.

Beaver Pond

Hop into the beaver pond,
a frosty winter shock.
Spring is not on time this year—
It must have lost its clock.

ō (silent e)

The Mole

The mole went down a little hole
and didn't make a sound.
She chose to be there all alone,
at home under the ground.

Elephant's Nose

Why do you suppose
    elephants have a hose
        for a nose?

Funny Joke

My baby brother poked a hole
into his eggy yoke.
The yoke exploded on his face—
It was a funny joke.

A Croaking Toad

A croaking toad on barren turf,
had made a goal to learn to surf.
He cut a surfboard out of toast,
and soared along the foamy coast.

All Aboard!

The train conductor loudly roared,
"Coaches loading...all aboard!"
The train went coasting—clack, clack, clack—
roaming down the railroad track.

-oi

My Disappointed Brother

My disappointed brother
could not avoid our bet.
Now he gets to sing my choice
of songs he will regret.

My Worm is Not a Noisy Pet

My worm is not a noisy pet
when curling in a coil.
It mostly likes to toil inside
the moisture of the soil.

-oo (moon)

The Zoo for the Drooling Goons

If you go to see the moon,
visit the zoo for the drooling goons.
They are not too ooky spooky,
but they are a little kooky.

Drooling goons like big balloons
and reading goofy moon cartoons.
With one tooth, they eat their goop,
drooling more with every scoop.

Zooming in lagoons of ooze,
makes them droopy for a snooze.
If you go to see the moon,
visit the zoo for the drooling goons.

(You will want to go back soon!)

−OO (good)

Little Red Riding Hood

When Red made cookies nice and hot
for Nana in the woods,
she saw a wolf down by the brook,
and ran off in her hood.

She quickly hoofed her way to Nan's
and looked inside her bed.
She stood by Nana's giant foot—
"You don't look good!" said Red.

"But you look good enough to cook!"
the Big Bad Wolf replied.
Red understood it was the wolf
and not her Nan inside.

So Red took cookies from her hood
and shook them on the bed.
The cookies hooked the Big Bad Wolf
and Red just quickly fled!

I Should Have

I should have cleaned my room today,
I should have washed the dishes,
I should have walked my little dog
and fed my three goldfishes.

I should have cleaned the litter box,
I should have made my bed,
I should have emptied out the trash
just like my mama said.

I should have finished all my chores,
I should have been all done.
I would have gotten out to play—
I could have had some fun.

-ou (out)

The Grouches

We are the grouches,
We don't want a mouse!
We only want grouches
around in our house!

We are the grouches,
and we like to pout.
We like to grumble
and grouse all about.

We are the grouches,
and we loudly shout,
"Get out, little mouse!
Get out, out, out, OUT!"

Howie

Howie is a big, brown owl
who prowls around at night.
Down he flies to catch some rats,
who cower down in fright.

The Crowning

The ladies dressed in flowered gowns,
and lords were bowing down.
The crowds in town had never seen
the crowning of a queen.

−OW (ō)

Snow Day

It's snowing out my window
and it's blowing very hard.
The snow is overflowing
into snowdrifts in my yard.

It's growing even higher,
a winter wonder show,
The snowman in my garden
likes it ten degrees below.

A snow day is a present,
an extra holiday,
I know I shouldn't grumble
that it came on Saturday.

The Crows

I hope those lowly crows have flown
    far, far away
        to parts unknown.

My Good Boy, Roy

He was a bit annoying,
my chewing little pup,
destroying all my favorite toys,
my mom made *me* clean up.

But now he is a good boy,
enjoying toys that squeak.
He doesn't chew my toys at all,
but licks me on the cheek.

He's such a loyal canine,
He never barks or whines,
A dog that's fit for royals—
I'm glad that Roy is mine.

-ph

My Elephant Ophelia

My elephant Ophelia
is phenomenally smart.
She counts up all the numbers
and then graphs them on a chart.

My elephant Ophelia
is like a symphony.
She likes to sing the alphabet
in microphones off-key.

My elephant Ophelia
walks high across the bars.
Now people take her photo—
She's become a superstar!

My elephant Ophelia
just makes me want to laugh,
when someone asks Ophelia
for her elephant autograph!

-pl

Platypus

When platypus is playing
in his playground in the brook,
he plunges under water
plucking fish without a hook.

His tail is like a beaver
with a duck bill on his face,
If it pleases you to see one,
then Australia is the place.

Platoon

Today I played all afternoon
with plastic army men,
I plotted with my green platoon
to plunder in the den.

-pr

Prehistoric Pet

I bought a prehistoric egg,
The price was pretty cheap.
The egg produced a dinosaur,
a present I could keep.

I call her Pretty Princess,
She likes to prance around,
But when she presses down her foot
it shakes me on the ground.

Her footprints are prodigious,
She probes into the sky,
I do predict she'll grow until
she is a mile high.

I take my Pretty Princess
to preschool with my friends.
They aren't surprised to see my pet—
because they can pretend.

-qu

The Queen's Quandary

The queen just made a strange request,
and quivered in her quandary.
She questioned me to show her how
to do the royal laundry.

The Quail

I gave a quarter to a quail
to make a quill out of her tail.
The quail just quacked...it was a duck—
and quibbled for another buck!

-sh

Sharkie

Three pirates on a shabby ship,
went sailing on a fishing trip.
They fished all day and fished all night,
but there was not a fish in sight.

Then in the shadows of the dark,
They saw a fish and shouted, "Shark!"
The shark pushed on the shabby ship,
and it began to shake and tip.

The ship went down with such a crash,
the pirates had to splish and splash!
When Sharkie saw the splashing crew—
she finished off some pirate stew!

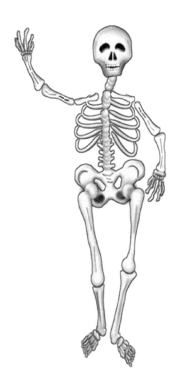

Skating Skeleton

I've seen a skating skeleton,
Alaska is his home.
He skates across so skillfully
the frozen ice of Gnome.

His skull is just a bony mask,
He hasn't any skin.
But he can skip and skim with ease—
the skating skeleton.

Sky

Skinny little whisker clouds
are skipping by the sun,
sketching purple through the sky
at dusk—when day is done.

-sl

Slug

A slug will slip and slide along
and leave a slimy trail.
It's even slower than a sloth
or sleepy little snail.

I Overslept This Morning

I overslept this morning,
my slumber was too deep,
until a sloppy, puppy kiss
awoke me from my sleep.

Slob

I am a little slovenly
and sluggish as a blob.
I sling my clothes upon the floor—
I am a teenage slob.

Sneezes

I'm sneezing great big sneezes,
I have the sniffles too,
I need my snowy snuggle bear,
ah-choo, ah-choo, ah-choo!

Snapshot

I snuck into my daddy's den
to watch him snore out loud.
I took a snapshot as he snoozed—
I'm sure he will be proud!

-sp

The Spider

The spider spins her web of lace,
which sparkles in her tiny space.
She is a splendid little spy,
when she spots her prey—the fly.

Aspen Tree

In the spring, the aspen tree
will sprout its wispy leaves.
Spinning little spots of green
will sputter in the eaves.

My Sister is a Constant Pest

My sister is a constant pest,
a blister on my toe.
She always sticks to me like glue,
no matter where I go.

Astronaut

I want to be an astronaut
and blast off into space,
to see some stars and asteroids,
or constellation face.

-tch

Witch's Batch

Never snatch a witch's batch
of rat with ketchup stew.
She will fetch her itching sauce
and pour it all on you!

When I Catch a Yucky Bug

When I catch a yucky bug,
I get a blotchy face.
I feel so wretched in my head,
I clutch my pillowcase.

Fletcher

Fletcher is an alley cat
with patches on his fur.
He catches lots of twitchy mice
and scratches when he purrs.

-th (the)

Bathing

When we're bathing in the tub,
we lather up our jaws.
We slather lather like a beard
to look like Santa Claus.

Another Brother

My mother says I get to have
another baby brother.
I'd rather get a puppy, please—
It plays more than the other.

-th _(three)

Birthday

Thursday is my birthday
and I'm thankful I am three!
It's thrilling blowing candles
on a cake meant just for me!

I've Been Playing in a Thicket

I've been playing in a thicket
on a very filthy path.
Something moved inside my hair—
I think I'll take a bath!

Treasure

Some pirates had some treasure
full of trinkets and some treats.
They traveled on the tropic sand
and tried to be discreet.

The pirates were triumphant,
They dug their pirate trap.
The trouble is that they forgot—
to make a treasure map!

My Own Tremendous Tree

I have my own tremendous tree
that I traverse up rapidly.
On straddled knees I swing with ease—
training for the high trapeze.

ŭ

Muddy Rubber Ducky

I put my rubber ducky
into a dumping truck,
We got to jump in puddles
and tumble in the muck.

We got a little grubby,
We had to scrub and scrub,
But we had fun together
with bubbles in the tub!

Grumpy Glum

Grumpy Glum is not much fun,
He grumbles in his mug.
Maybe Grumpy Glum just needs
a cuddle and a hug.

Duke

He used to be a puppy,
so tiny and so cute.
But Duke is getting rather huge—
a slobber making brute.

My Paper Flute

I used some tubes of cardboard,
and lots of super glue.
I made a special little flute
and played a tune for you.

-ur

The Purple Glurple

It's urgent you don't turn around.
Just hurry and don't make a sound.
There's something big and extra burly,
with a wig that's extra curly.

It slurps and burps its glurpy food,
and seems to be in quite a mood.
The purple glurple says it's tame—
better scurry just the same.

Burt

Burt is such a curious
and sturdy little turtle.
He must be sure he knows his way—
since turning is a hurdle.

Killer Whales

What can cartwheel on the sea?
Whistle underneath with glee?
Whales of black and white have flair,
when they leap into the air.

It Begins as a Whisper

It begins as whisper
and whistles through the air.
The whirling wind is whining
and whipping everywhere.
Whoosh!

-wr

Secret Diary

Inside her secret diary
my sister wrote a song.
But when she wrote I was a pest,
I wrote back, "Hey, you're wrong!"

I am **NOT**
a Pest !

I Wrestled with a Rhino

I wrestled with a rhino.
I wriggled with a snake.
I wrapped it all around my neck—
That was a big mistake.

T-Rex

He didn't get much exercise
when chasing dino treats,
but T-Rex had the luxury
of eating extra meat.

He always got excited,
His goal was so succinct,
He was an expert hunter—
until he went extinct!

Baxter Made a Mixture

Baxter made a mixture,
The texture was like wax.
He packed it in his lunchbox,
and ate it for his snacks.

The Chickens Were Relaxing

The chickens were relaxing
inside their comfy box.
They never were expecting
to see a hungry fox.

-y (ī)

My Dinner Makes Me Want to Cry

My dinner makes me want to cry
and I will tell you why.
I do not want to try my peas—
I'd rather eat a fly.

My Parrot

My parrot isn't shy at all
when flying in the sky.
He will reply to everyone,
"Hello, hello, goodbye!"

The Wright Brothers

Why did Orville try and try?
Why did Wilbur too?
They had to try and reach the sky,
to fly as birdies do.

I Have a Lucky Penny

I have a lucky penny,
all shiny and brand new.
It's just a little slimy
inside my smelly shoe.

Floppy

Floppy is my furry pet,
a fuzzy little bunny.
When she hops inside my lap,
I think she's really funny.

Sloppy Joes

Sloppy Joes are messy,
and sticky on my face,
but they just make me happy,
any time or place.

Made in the USA
Lexington, KY
24 May 2018